VALUE BUILDERS

CONVICTION & SINCERITY

Bible-based activities to strengthen Christian values

All puzzles and Bible activities are based on the NIV.

ISBN: 0-7814-5102-7

Edited by Debbie Bible
Book Design by Jack Rogers
Cover Illustration by Corbin Hillam
Interior Illustrations by Dana Regan & Corbin Hillam

VALUE BUILDERS
CONVICTION & SINCERITY

TABLE OF CONTENTS

INTRODUCTION FOR ADULT FRIENDS OF CHILDREN

(Parents, Teachers, and Other Friends of Children)

Values. What are they? How do we acquire them? Can we change them?

"Values" is a popular term, usually meaning *the standard that governs how one acts and conducts one's life*. Our personal standards, or values, are learned and adapted, possibly changed and relearned, over a lifetime of experiences and influences.

Children begin acquiring personal values at birth. As parents, teachers, and other adults who love children, we are concerned that they are learning worthwhile values, rather than being randomly influenced by everything around them. By God's design, we cannot control the process of acquiring values, but we can influence the process in a variety of ways. Our consistent modeling of biblical values is a vital influence, but children must also be encouraged to talk about specific values and be aware of these values in action in themselves and others.

These biblical values are God's values. He has established His standards to help us know how to live our lives and how we are to treat other people. Our goal is to have these biblical values be a part of each child's experience.

A value becomes one's own when a person chooses to act on that value consistently. Saying that we hold to the value of honesty, yet bending the truth or telling a lie when pressured, is a contradiction.

Providing opportunities for children to investigate a specific value, identifying with people in the Bible who have that value, and trying to put it into practice in real life situations will help strengthen the value in the lives of the children and reinforce its importance. The purpose of the Value Builders Series is to provide such opportunities.

This book in the Value Builders Series focuses on **having conviction** and **showing sincerity**. Having conviction is *showing that what you believe is important to you.* Jesus showed His conviction about the temple when He demanded that the money changers, merchants, and animals leave the temple court. Shadrach, Meshach, and Abednego are also examples of people having conviction. They stood before King Nebuchadnezzar, explaining that they would not serve his gods, even though they knew he would then have them thrown into a blazing fiery furnace.

Showing sincerity is *saying and doing what is true without pretending or hiding anything.* Jairus came to Jesus in sincerity as he asked Jesus to come to his home to heal his daughter. Timothy lived a life with sincere faith and genuine character.

CONVICTION & SINCERITY

The Value Builders Series provides Bible story activities, craft activities, and life application activities that focus on specific biblical values. These books can be used by children working alone, or the pages can be reproduced and used in a classroom setting.

In a classroom setting, this book could be used to supplement curriculum that you are using, or it can be used as a curriculum itself in a 30-55 minute period. Each page is coded at the bottom to suggest where it might fit in a teaching session. The codes are as follows:

= Definition page
= Bible Story page
= Craft page
= Life Application page

Some suggestions for using the materials in this book in a 30-55 minute period are:

5-10 minutes:	Introduce the value and discuss the definition. Use pages entitled, "What Is Conviction?" or "What Is Sincerity?"
10-15 minutes:	Present one of the Bible stories, using appropriate pages. Encourage the children to describe what it might have been like to be in that situation and what other things could have happened.
10-20 minutes:	Choose life application activity pages or craft activities that are appropriate to the children in your class. Design some group applications for the pages you have chosen.
5-10 minutes:	To conclude, use the page entitled, "The Value of Conviction" or "The Value of Sincerity" and encourage the children to make a commitment to focus on this value for the next few days or weeks. Pray for God's help to guide the children as they learn to live by His standards.

WHAT IS CONVICTION?

VALUE BUILDERS
CONVICTION & SINCERITY

CONVICTION IS... **showing that what you believe is important to you.**

I think conviction can also mean ______________________________

____

You show what is important to you by your

actions frown smile attitude friends words

✎ **Circle the words in the word search.**

B	F	R	I	E	N	D	S
W	C	F	F	G	L	S	B
O	M	Q	J	R	M	B	D
R	A	C	T	I	O	N	S
D	F	K	L	W	C	W	N
S	F	E	K	D	M	W	N
A	T	T	I	T	U	D	E

Conviction is important to me.
When I show that what I believe is important to me, then conviction becomes one of my values.

Name ______________________________

Date ______________________________

God's values are the STANDARD to help me know how to live my life and treat other people

THE BIBLE TELLS ABOUT CONVICTION

Jesus Shows Conviction about the Temple

John 2:13-16

When it was almost time for the Jewish Passover, Jesus went up to Jerusalem. In the temple courts [Court of the Gentiles] he found men selling cattle, sheep and doves, and others sitting at tables exchanging money. So he made a whip out of cords, and drove all from the temple area, both sheep and cattle; he scattered the coins of the money changers and overturned their tables. To those who sold doves he said, "Get these out of here! How dare you turn my Father's house into a market!"

"EXCHANGING MONEY" MEANS THEY WERE TRADING THEIR MONEY FOR THE KIND THAT WAS USED THERE.

✎ **Put a check by the right answer for each.**

The temple is like a

___ church.

___ store.

The men were

___ praying and worshiping God.

___ selling animals and exchanging money.

When Jesus said the temple was His Father's house, He meant

___ it was God's house.

___ it was a place where people live.

Jesus showed He had conviction about God's house when He

___ didn't do anything about the wrong things that were going on.

___ made the money changers and the people with the animals leave.

THE BIBLE TELLS ABOUT CONVICTION

Jesus Shows Conviction about the Temple

✎ **Read about Jesus in your Bible in John 2:13-16 or on page 6. After you read the Bible story fill in the words.**

angry	cattle	doves	leave	market
money	sheep	tables	temple	whip

1. Jesus went to the ____________________ and saw people selling animals such as ____________________ , ____________________ , and ____________________.

2. Other men were exchanging the ____________________________ so people could buy the animals.

3. Jesus made a ________________ and made the animals get out of the temple area.

4. Jesus turned the ____________________ upside down. He told the people who were selling the doves to ____________________.

5. Jesus was _______________________ because the people were using God's house like a ____________________.

✎ **Choose one of the sentences about the story and draw a picture of it.**

THE BIBLE TELLS ABOUT CONVICTION

Jesus Shows Conviction about the Temple

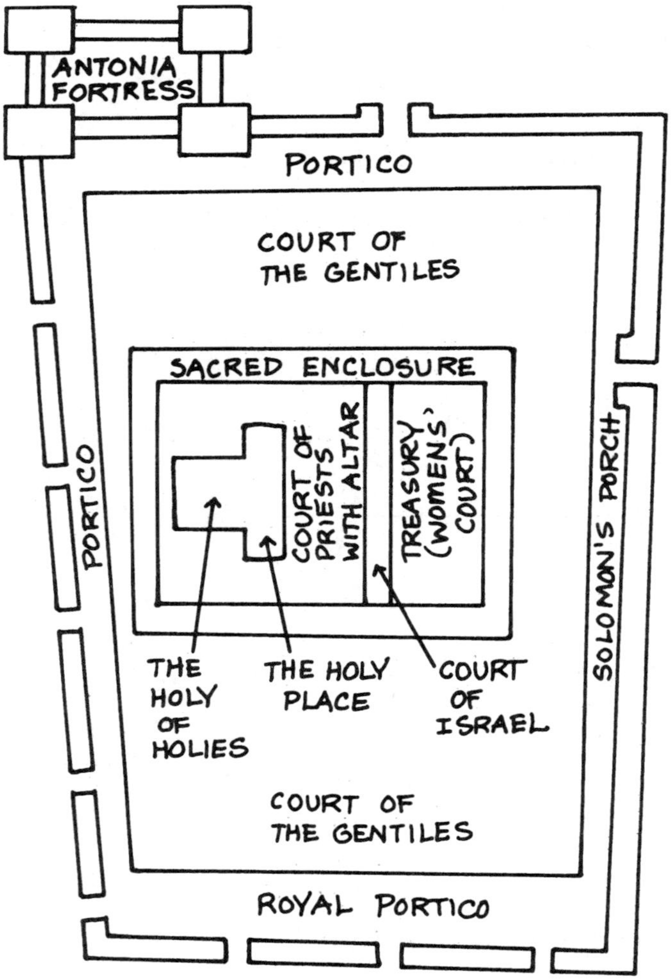

Read about Jesus in your Bible in John 2:13-16 or on page 6.

Jesus made the animals and money changers leave the temple. They were in the Court of the Gentiles.

Here is a layout showing where different things would be on the inside.

✎ **Put an X on the place where Jesus met the money changers.**
✎ **Color the Court of the Gentiles orange.**
✎ **Color the Women's Court blue.**

Here is a picture of what the temple might have looked like from the outside.
✎ **Color the picture.**

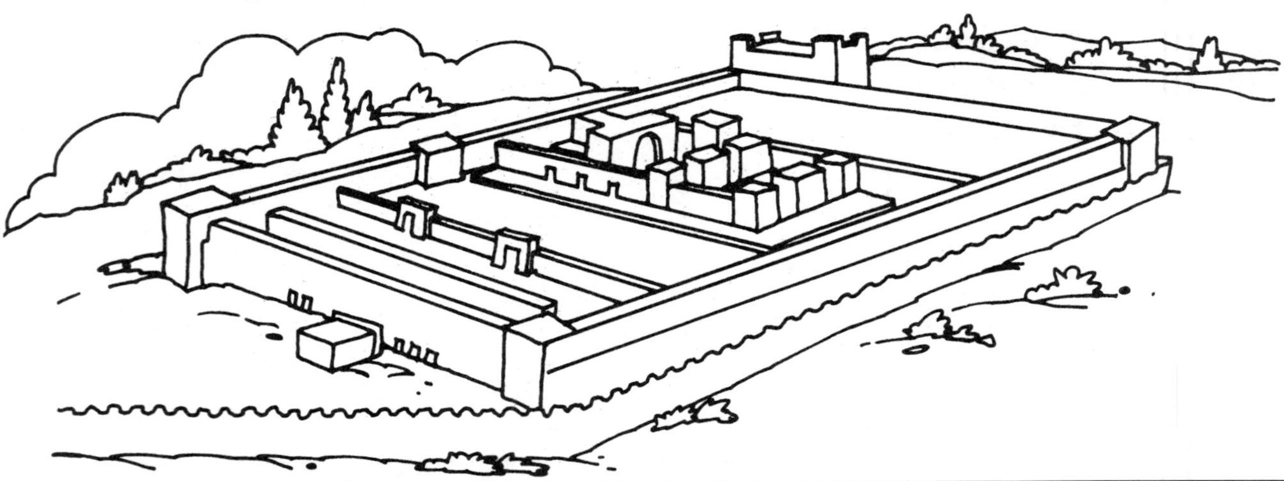

IF SOMEONE WANTS YOU TO DO WRONG

VALUE BUILDERS
CONVICTION & SINCERITY

✎ **On each line, write the letter that comes BEFORE the letter you see under the line. When you have solved the code, write each word in the crossword puzzle.**

The Bible verse in Deuteronomy 13:6-8 says,

If your very own ___ ___ ___ ___ ___ ___ ___ . . . or your
c s p u i f s

___ ___ ___ ___ ___ ___ ___ friend
d m p t f t u

___ ___ ___ ___ ___ ___ ___ ___ entices you, saying, "Let us
t f d s f u m z

___ ___ and ___ ___ ___ ___ ___ ___ ___ other gods". . . do not
h p x p s t i j q

yield to him or ___ ___ ___ ___ ___ ___ to him. Show him no
m j t u f o

___ ___ ___ ___ . Do not spare him or ___ ___ ___ ___ ___ ___ him.
q j u z t i j f m e

"ENTICES" MEANS SOMEONE IS TRYING TO TALK YOU INTO DOING SOMETHING.

This verse is about not letting others talk you into doing what's wrong. If you were explaining this verse to your friend, what would you say?

____

____

____

"YIELD" MEANS TO GIVE IN.

SOME IMPORTANT THINGS TO DO

✎ **Conviction is showing that what you believe is important to you. Finish drawing the pictures that show what is important to you.**

YOU ARE IMPORTANT TO ME. HOLD STILL WHILE I DRAW YOU.

MAKE A BOX AND WRITE YOUR CONVICTIONS

Make a paper box and then show your friends how to make one. Make a list of six things you believe and write them on the sides of the box (one to a side). This will help to remind you how important they are.

You need:

- ☐ A square piece of paper about 8-1/2" x 8-1/2"
- ☐ Felt-tip markers

✂ **To make a Box:**

1. Fold the paper in half, and then fold it in half again (to make 4 squares).
2. Fold it diagonally, from one corner to another. Open it up so it has only the first fold still in place.
3. Start at the fold (as shown) and push each side inward to make an inverted fold. Press the folds down firmly. (Your paper now looks like a triangle with a point at the top.)
4. Fold each bottom corner of the front piece up to touch the top. Turn the paper over and do the same.
5. Fold the front side points in to touch the center. Turn the paper over and do the same.
6. Fold down the top points and tuck them into the open end of the small triangles just below them. Do the same on the back.
7. Blow hard into the hole at one end to make the box take shape.
8. Write some of the things that are important to you on the sides of the box.

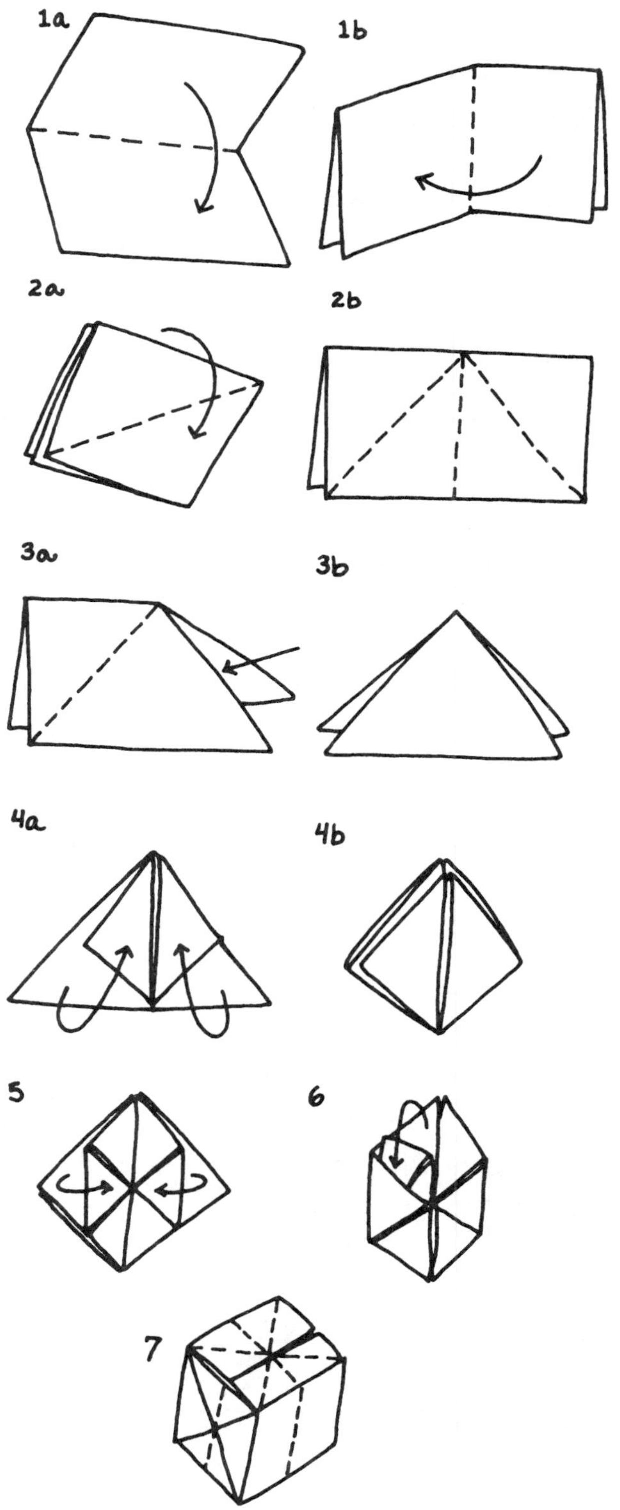

FRIENDS AND HAVING CONVICTION

✎ **What do you tell your friends about what you believe? What would you say to these kids? Write your answers.**

What could Lynn say to her friends?

What could Gary say to his friends?

What could Valerie say to her friends?

OBEYING GOD IS SHOWING YOUR CONVICTION

VALUE BUILDERS
CONVICTION & SINCERITY

✎ **Use some of the words in the Bible verse, Acts 4:19-20, to find out an important thing for you to do. Write the letters of the word with the same number on the blanks. The first one is done for you.**

But Peter and John replied, "Judge (13) for yourselves (6) whether (15) it is
right (2) in God's sight (12) to obey (9) you rather (11) than God. (5) For (8) we cannot (4)
help (7) speaking (3) about what (14) we have seen (1) and heard (10)."

1. S E E N
2. ___ ___ ___ ___ ___
3. ___ ___ ___ ___ ___ ___ ___ ___
4. ___ ___ ___ ___ ___ ___
5. ___ ___ ___
6. ___ ___ ___ ___ ___ ___ ___ ___ ___ ___
7. ___ ___ ___ ___
8. ___ ___ ___
9. ___ ___ ___ ___
10. ___ ___ ___ ___ ___
11. ___ ___ ___ ___ ___ ___
12. ___ ___ ___ ___ ___
13. ___ ___ ___ ___ ___
14. ___ ___ ___ ___
15. ___ ___ ___ ___ ___ ___ ___

✎ **Write the letters from the box in order here.**

___ ___ ___ ___ ___   ___ ___   ___ ___ ___   ___ ___ ___ ___ ___

What is one thing you will choose to do to obey God, no matter what?

____

VALUE BUILDERS
CONVICTION & SINCERITY

THE BIBLE TELLS ABOUT CONVICTION

Three Men Have Conviction about Serving God

Daniel 3:1-28

King Nebuchadnezzar made an image of gold, ninety feet high and nine feet wide . . .

Then the herald loudly proclaimed, "This is what you are commanded to do, O peoples, nations and men of every language: As soon as you hear the sound of the horn, flute, zither, lyre, harp, pipes and all kinds of music, you must fall down and worship the image of gold that King Nebuchadnezzar has set up. Whoever does not fall down and worship will immediately be thrown into a blazing furnace."

. . . Therefore . . . all the peoples . . . fell down and worshiped the image of gold that King Nebuchadnezzar had set up.

At this time some . . . said to King Nebuchadnezzar, "O king . . . there are some Jews whom you have set over the affairs of the province of Babylon—Shadrach, Meshach and Abednego—who pay no attention to you, O king. They neither serve your gods nor worship the image of gold you have set up."

Furious with rage, Nebuchadnezzar summoned Shadrach, Meshach and Abednego. So these men were brought before the king, and Nebuchadnezzar said to them, "Is it true, Shadrach, Meshach and Abednego . . . ? If you do not worship it, you will be thrown immediately into a blazing furnace. Then what god will be able to rescue you from my hand?"

Shadrach, Meshach and Abednego replied to the king, "O Nebuchadnezzar, we do not need to defend ourselves before you in this matter. If we are thrown into the blazing furnace, the God we serve is able to save us from it, and he will rescue us from your hand, O king. But even if he does not, we want you to know, O king, that we will not serve your gods or worship the image of gold you have set up."

(Read the rest of this story on page 15)

✎ **Use the code to find out what Shadrach, Meshach, and Abednego told the King.**

Our ______________ (8-5-11) can ______________ (3-12-1-10) us from ______________ (9-7-4-10).

No ______________ (6-12-2-2-10-4) what, we will not ______________ (3-10-4-1-10)

your ______________ (8-5-11-3) or image.

CODE:

1 = V	2 = T	3 = S	4 = R
5 = O	6 = M	7 = I	8 = G
9 = F	10 = E	11 = D	12 = A

THE BIBLE TELLS ABOUT CONVICTION

Three Men Have Conviction about Serving God

(Daniel 3:1-28 continued from page 14)

"FURIOUS" MEANS VERY, VERY ANGRY.

Then Nebuchadnezzar was furious. . . . He ordered the furnace heated seven times hotter than usual and commanded some of the strongest soldiers in his army to tie up Shadrach, Meshach and Abednego and throw them into the blazing furnace. . . . The furnace [was] so hot that the flames of the fire killed the soldiers who took up Shadrach, Meshach and Abednego, and these three men, firmly tied, fell into the blazing furnace.

Then King Nebuchadnezzar leaped to his feet in amazement and asked his advisers, "Weren't there three men that we tied up and threw into the fire?" They replied, "Certainly, O king."

He said, "Look! I see four men walking around in the fire, unbound and unharmed, and the fourth looks like a son of the gods."

Nebuchadnezzar then approached the opening of the blazing furnace and shouted, "Shadrach, Meshach and Abednego, servants of the Most High God, come out! Come here!"

So Shadrach, Meshach and Abednego came out of the fire, and [everyone] crowded around them. They saw that the fire had not harmed their bodies, nor was a hair of their heads singed; their robes were not scorched, and there was no smell of fire on them.

Then Nebuchadnezzar said, "Praise be to the God of Shadrach, Meshach and Abednego . . . [They] were willing to give up their lives rather than serve or worship any god except their own God. . . . No other god can save in this way."

✎ **Draw lines to finish each sentence.**

1. The king ordered all the people	to worship someone who is not our God.
2. Shadrach, Meshach, and Abednego said it was wrong	put in the fire.
3. The king had the three men	praised God.
4. In the furnace, the three men	to worship someone who is not our God.
5. When he saw that the men were not burned, the king	were not burned at all.

THE BIBLE TELLS ABOUT CONVICTION

Three Men Have Conviction about Serving God

Read about the conviction of these three men in your Bible in Daniel 3:1-28 or on pages 14 and 15.

✎ **Write the answers to these questions in the crossword puzzle.**

1. What is the king's name?

2. Who were killed by the fire?

3, 4, and 5. What are the names of the men who would not bow down?

6. What was ninety feet high and nine feet wide?

7. Where was the fire?

8. What was the signal for the people to bow?

✎ **What do you think? Circle YES or NO.**

YES NO It was easy to say "NO, we won't" to the king.

YES NO If you knew you would be laughed at or lose a friend, you would still stand by your convictions about God.

YES NO If you knew the other kids would laugh at you, you would still refuse to go along with something that is wrong.

YES NO Some things are so important that people have been willing to die for what they believed.

PUPPETS FOR A PLAY ABOUT CONVICTION

Make puppets to use with the puppet play on pages 20 and 21.

You need:

- ☐ 14 or more 4-1/2" paper rolls
- ☐ Markers or crayons
- ☐ White glue
- ☐ (3) 12" pieces of string to tie Shadrach, Meshach, and Abednego

✂ **To make Puppets:**

1. Make copies of the puppet patterns.
2. To make Shadrach, Meshach, and Abednego you have one puppet pattern. You will need to make more. Color each one differently. Do the same for the officials, soldiers, and people in the crowd.
3. Cut out the puppets and glue each to a separate paper roll. Make sure you do not glue the arms.

KING

FOURTH PERSON

PUPPETS FOR A PLAY ABOUT CONVICTION

SOLDIER

OFFICIAL

CROWD PERSON

SHADRACH
MESHACH
ABEDNEGO

PROPS TO USE WITH THE PUPPET PLAY

VALUE BUILDERS
CONVICTION & SINCERITY

Shadrach, Meshach, and Abednego told King Nebuchadnezzar that they would not bow to the image no matter what happened to them. They would only worship and honor the Lord. When you use this image in your puppet play, you can see how tall the image would have been compared to the size of your puppet people!

You need:

- ☐ 5 paper grocery bags
- ☐ Scissors, stapler, and ruler
- ☐ Newspaper and a black marker
- ☐ Gold and grey or black spray paint

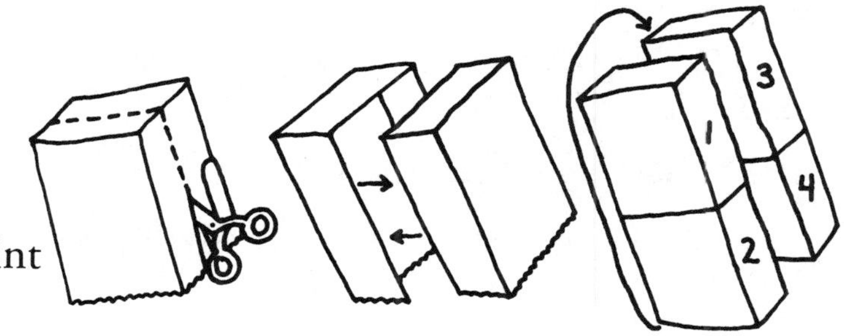

To make the Image:

1. Cut four of the grocery bags in half lengthwise, as shown, and slide one half inside the other to make four tall, narrow blocks, about 7" x 17" each.
2. Staple the side edges of each block to hold the two pieces of bag together.
3. Crumple several sheets of newspaper and put them inside one of the paper blocks. Use this as the base or bottom section of your image.
4. Add another paper block by slipping it over the edges of the top of the base block with about 2" of overlap. Tape it in place.
5. Add the other two blocks in the same way, so you have a tall column about 60" high. You may want to add a small amount of newspaper to the top part of the column before taping, but be careful not to make it top heavy.
6. Paint the image with gold paint. Allow time for the paint to dry and then use it for your puppet play.

To make the Furnace:

1. Cut the grocery bag so that when you stand it up it measures 14" tall.
2. Stand the bag upside down and cut an opening in one side of the bag about 6" high and 4-1/2" wide.
3. With the bag standing upside down, cut a 5" circle from the bottom. This will be the top of the furnace.
4. Paint the furnace grey and allow time for the paint to dry.
5. Use the black marker to draw the outline of large stones on the outside of the bag.

VALUE BUILDERS
CONVICTION & SINCERITY

BEING TRUE TO GOD IN A BURNING FURNACE

A Puppet Play Based on Daniel 3:1-28

The people in this story are: King Nebuchadnezzar, Shadrach, Meshach, Abednego, fourth person in furnace, royal officials (two or more), soldiers (three or more), and people (four or more).

PREPARATION:
1. Follow the directions for making the puppets on page 17 and the image and furnace on page 19.

SETTING: This takes place in Babylon, in the plain of Dura.

Put the image to the left of the stage with KING NEBUCHADNEZZAR standing near, and the OFFICIALS and SOLDIERS beside him. Put the furnace to the far right.

OFFICIAL #1 *(loudly)*: This is what you are commanded to do, O peoples, nations, and men of every language. As soon as you hear the sound of the horn, flute, zither, lyre, harp, pipes, and all kinds of music, you must fall down and worship the image of gold that King Nebuchadnezzar has set up. Whoever does not fall down and worship will immediately be thrown into a blazing furnace.

[OFFICIAL #1 holds hand to mouth as if blowing a trumpet and makes the sound of music. PEOPLE and SHADRACH, MESHACH, and ABEDNEGO enter. Everyone bows to the image except SHADRACH, MESHACH, AND ABEDNEGO.]

OFFICIAL #2 *(walks over to the king)*: O king, you made a law that as soon as we heard the music we were to worship this image, or we would be thrown into the furnace. Well, look, over there, see? Shadrach, Meshach, and Abednego aren't worshiping this golden statue.

KING *(angrily calls)*: Is it true, Shadrach, Meshach, and Abednego? Aren't you bowing to the statue? This time, when you hear the music, bow down! If you don't, you will be thrown into the furnace. Do you think any god could rescue you then?

ABEDNEGO *(walks up to the king with MESHACH beside him and speaks quietly and calmly)*: O Nebuchadnezzar, if you throw us into the fire, the God we serve can save us from burning up. But even if God does not save us from the fire, we still will not worship your gods.

KING *(even more angry, speaks to the soldiers)*: Heat the furnace seven times hotter than it usually is! Get someone to tie up these three men and throw them into the fire!

SOLDERS go over to the furnace and throw fuel inside it, while other SOLDIERS go to SHADRACH, MESHACH, and ABEDNEGO, tie them up, and lead them to the furnace. As they approach the furnace, the soldiers all fall dead because the fire is too hot, and SHADRACH, MESHACH and ABEDNEGO fall into the furnace.]

BEING TRUE TO GOD IN A BURNING FURNACE

VALUE BUILDERS
CONVICTION & SINCERITY

KING *(jumps to his feet in surprise as FOURTH PERSON moves into the furnace as SHADRACH, MESHACH and ABEDNEGO stand up, untied)*: Didn't the soldiers just throw three men into the fire?

OFFICIAL #1: Certainly, O king.

KING *(pointing to the furnace)*: I see four men in there, and not one of them is burning or tied up. One of them looks like he is someone divine! *(Walks over to the furnace and shouts into it)* Shadrach, Meshach, and Abednego, come out of that furnace!

[FOURTH PERSON leaves, SHADRACH, MESHACH, and ABEDNEGO walk to the king. Everyone crowds around, reaching out to touch their hair and clothes.]

OFFICIAL #2 *(whispering)*: I can't believe it! Their clothes aren't even burned.

KING *(loudly, to all)*: Praise to the God of Shadrach, Meshach, and Abednego, who has sent an angel and rescued them. They trusted in God even when it looked like they would die for it. There is no other god like this. This is the REAL God. I now make a new law: Anyone who says anything against the God of Shadrach, Meshach, and Abednego will be killed. *(To Shadrach, Meshach, and Abednego)* I know how powerful your God is, and how much you trust Him to help you do what is right. I want you to do some of the important jobs in my country.

[SHADRACH, MESHACH, and ABEDNEGO walk toward the front of the stage.]

SHADRACH: Did you see how everyone was so interested in the power of God and how He saved us from the fire?

MESHACH: It was difficult to stand there when everyone else was bowing down. I could tell that everyone was peeking at us. I was really getting scared. But even when the king was mad and yelling at us, I knew we were doing the right thing.

ABEDNEGO: If we had kept our faith in God a secret, and just bowed down, what do you think would have happened?

SHADRACH: No one would have known how powerful our God really is. The people certainly had a chance to find out what God can do when His children need Him.

MESHACH: I'm so glad I serve God, but I really don't like going into that furnace. Did you? *[ALL exit.]*

WHEN YOU HAVE CONVICTION

✎ **Use these clues to remind yourself what conviction is. Write the letters on the lines to match the numbers.**

First word:

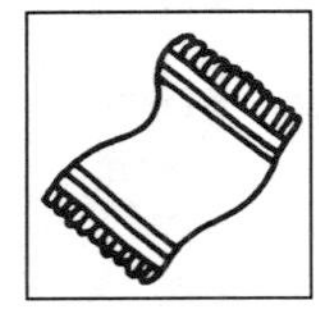

1. My first letter is in BUG, but not in RUG.
2. My second letter is in TREE, but not in TRY.

3. My third letter is in BELT, but not in BEET.
4. My fourth letter is in ICE, but not in ROSE.

5. My fifth letter is in EEL, but not in LOAF.
6. My sixth letter is in VELVET, but not in LETTER.
7. My seventh letter is in SHOULDER, but not in SHOULD.

Second word:

1. My first letter is in YES, but not in GUESS.

2. My second letter is in NO, but not in KNEW.
3. My third letter is in TURN, but not in TERN.

CONVICTION is showing that what you ___ ___ ___ ___ ___ ___ ___
(1 2 3 4 5 6 7)

is IMPORTANT to ___ ___ ___ .
(1 2 3)

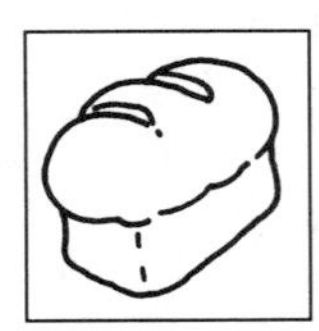

✎ **Put an X by the things that are important to you.**

_____ Believing that Jesus is God's Son.

_____ Doing things the way God teaches is the right way.

_____ Going to church and reading the Bible.

_____ Telling others about Jesus.

THE VALUE OF CONVICTION

God's values are the STANDARD to help me to know how to live my life and treat other people

HOW CAN YOU KNOW WHAT YOUR VALUES ARE? Look at the things you DO, SAY, and THINK. If you spend time doing something, then you know it is one of your values.

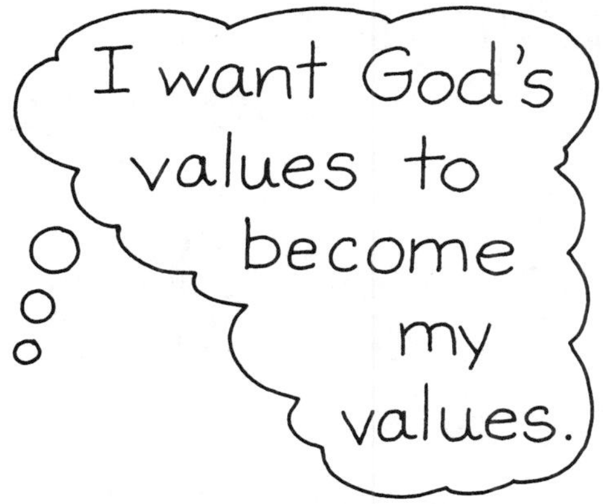

✎ **Draw a picture of yourself here.** Are you thinking what is in the thought balloon?

My name is ______________________________

Conviction ____________ important to me.
(is / is not)

I ____________ spend time showing that what I believe is important to me.
(do / do not)

Showing that what I believe is important to me is conviction.

I can show that conviction is becoming my value when I ____________________

____________________ and ____________________

✎ **Use fabric paint to decorate a sweatshirt that will help you to share one of your convictions about God.**

WHAT IS SINCERITY?

SINCERITY IS . . . **saying and doing what is true without pretending or hiding anything.**

I think sincerity can also mean ____

____

✎ **Circle YES or NO if you think these are sincere things to say.**

YES NO

YES NO

YES NO

YES NO

Being sincere is important to me.
When I spend time doing and saying what is true, without pretending or hiding anything, then sincerity becomes one of my values.

Name ______________________________

Date ______________________________

God's values are the STANDARD to help me know how to live my life and treat other people

THE BIBLE TELLS ABOUT SINCERITY

VALUE BUILDERS
CONVICTION & SINCERITY

Jairus Asks for Jesus' Help

Mark 5:21-43

When Jesus had again crossed over by boat to the other side of the lake, a large crowd gathered around him while he was by the lake. Then one of the synagogue rulers, named Jairus, came there. Seeing Jesus, he fell at his feet and pleaded earnestly with him, "My little daughter is dying. Please come and put your hands on her so that she will be healed and live." So Jesus went with him.

A "SYNAGOGUE RULER" IS THE LEADER OF THE SYNAGOGUE, A BUILDING LIKE A CHURCH BUILDING.

JAIRUS WAS IN CHARGE OF WHAT THE PEOPLE DID IN THE SYNAGOGUE.

A large crowd followed and pressed around him. . . .

While Jesus was still speaking, some men came from the house of Jairus, the synagogue ruler. "Your daughter is dead," they said. "Why bother the teacher any more?"

Ignoring what they said, Jesus told the synagogue ruler, "Don't be afraid; just believe."

(Read the rest of this story on page 26)

✎ **Choose the right words to finish each sentence. You will need to read the entire story (including page 26) first.**

1. The girl was ______________________ .
   very sick just pretending

2. The girl was ______________________ .
   3 years old 12 years old

3. Jairus was ______________________ when he asked Jesus to come to heal his daughter.
   sincere just pretending.

4. Jairus wanted his daughter to ______________________ .
   keep being sick be well

5. Jesus asked Jairus ______________________ .
   to believe to be sad.

THE BIBLE TELLS ABOUT SINCERITY

Jairus Asks for Jesus' Help

(Mark 5:21-43 continued from page 25)

He did not let anyone follow him except Peter, James and John the brother of James. When they came to the home of the synagogue ruler, Jesus saw a commotion, with people crying and wailing loudly. He went in and said to them, "Why all this commotion and wailing? The child is not dead but asleep." But they laughed at him.

After he put them all out, he took the child's father and mother and the disciples who were with him, and went in where the child was. He took her by the hand and said to her, "Talitha koum!" (which means, "Little girl, I say to you, get up!"). Immediately the girl stood up and walked around (she was twelve years old). At this they were completely astonished. He gave strict orders not to let anyone know about this, and told them to give her something to eat.

"WAILING LOUDLY" MEANS TO CRY LOUDLY. SOME PEOPLE WOULD CRY THIS WAY AS AN HONOR TO THE ONE WHO HAD DIED.

✎ **Draw a line to show who said these words.**

"My little daughter is dying."

Jairus

"Why bother the teacher any more?"

"Your daughter is dead."

some men

"Don't be afraid; just believe."

"Please come . . . so that she will be healed and live."

"The child is not dead but asleep."

Jesus

"Little girl, get up!"

THE BIBLE TELLS ABOUT SINCERITY

Jairus Asks for Jesus' Help

Read Mark 5:21-43 in your Bible or on pages 25 and 26. ✎ **Write a number under each picture to show what happened first, second, and so on. Draw in the missing pictures.**

_____
Jesus and Jairus started walking to Jairus' house.

1
Jairus asked Jesus to come to his house and heal his daughter.

_____
Some men said that Jairus' daughter had already died and not to bother Jesus.

_____
They came to Jairus' house and saw the people crying loudly.

_____
Jesus told Jairus not to be afraid and to believe.

_____
The girl stood up and walked around.

_____
They went into the room where the girl was lying.

_____
Jesus held the girl's hand and told her to get up.

Value Builders
CONVICTION & SINCERITY

SINCERE FROM MORNING UNTIL NIGHT

✎ **Follow Dan through his day by going through the maze. Look for ways he can be sincere. Perhaps this will help you to think of ways you can be sincere, too!**

SINCERITY WITH OTHER PEOPLE

Romans 12:9

✎ **Do the math in the code box. Each answer will be the code for the letter. Write the matching letters below to discover the Bible verse.**

CODE BOX:

2 + 2 = ____ = B

6 - 3 = ____ = C

7 + 7 = ____ = E

2 - 1 = ____ = I

1 + 1 = ____ = L

9 - 2 = ____ = M

3 + 2 = ____ = N

5 + 5 = ____ = O

6 + 6 = ____ = R

10 -1 = ____ = S

8 + 8 = ____ = T

7 - 1 = ____ = U

4 + 4 = ____ = V

____ ____ ____ ____ ____ ____ ____ ____ ____ ____
2 10 8 14 7 6 9 16 4 14

____ ____ ____ ____ ____ ____ ____ .
9 1 5 3 14 12 14

What can you do to show someone you love them in a sincere way?

____

GIVE A SINCERE GIFT OF MUDDY MIX

Gifts are a wonderful way to show your sincerity and love. Make this Muddy Mix and give some to a special friend.

You need:

- ☐ Small package of chocolate sandwich cookies
- ☐ 1 quart-size plastic bag (zips to lock)
- ☐ 1 small (3 oz.) package of instant chocolate pudding
- ☐ 2 cups milk
- ☐ 8-oz. carton of whipped dessert topping
- ☐ 2 teaspoons sugar
- ☐ 1 small (3 oz.) package of light cream cheese, softened
- ☐ Large and small mixing bowls
- ☐ Mixing spoon
- ☐ 4 or 5 clear plastic cups, 6-oz. size

To make Muddy Mix:

1. Put the chocolate sandwich cookies in the plastic bag, close tightly, and crush the cookies into very small pieces.
2. Stir the milk and pudding together in the large bowl. Continue stirring until smooth.
3. Add the whipped topping and mix together thoroughly.
4. In the small mixing bowl, thoroughly blend the sugar and the cream cheese.
5. Add the cream cheese mixture to the pudding. Stir well.
6. Put a small amount of the cookie crumbs in the bottom of each plastic cup.
7. Add about 1/2 cup of the pudding mixture to each cup, and put additional cookie crumbs on the top.

BEING SINCERE INSTEAD OF COVERING UP

VALUE BUILDERS
CONVICTION & SINCERITY

✎ **The letters you need to solve this puzzle are hidden inside many other letters. Write the correct letters on the blanks. HINT: The letters you need will always be in triplets!**

To be sincere . . .

1. ___ ___ ___ ___ A A S S S M T T T Y O O O J J I P P P

and

___ ___ ___ ___ ___ T T T B B H H H I I I A N N N C K K K

___ ___ ___ ___ ___ ___ OBBBPPEEEFFFUOOOMMRRRWEEEXX

you say something.

2. Ask ___ ___ ___ M M Y G G G C C O O O Q S S D D D P

to ___ ___ ___ ___ H H H J J E E E I N N L L L P P P

___ ___ ___ N N Q Y Y Y K O O O D D U U U W

know the right thing to say.

3. Ask yourself these questions about what you say to others:

✎ **Mark YES or NO.**

YES	NO	
____	____	Are my words true?
____	____	Do I mean what I say?
____	____	Am I just saying something nice to someone because I want something in return?
____	____	Am I trying to hide something?

VALUE BUILDERS
CONVICTION & SINCERITY

BE SINCERE IN WHAT YOU THINK

Be careful what you think about! It can either help or hurt your ability to be sincere. ✎ **Read Philippians 4:8 in your Bible, and then figure out the code to discover the types of thoughts that can help you grow in sincerity. In the ☐ draw a picture of yourself or write your name.**

"NOBLE" MEANS IT'S THE BEST, THE HIGHEST VALUE.

Is it ____ ____ ____ ____ ?
✰ ✳ ✼ ✥

Is it ____ ____ ____ ____ ?
✶ ✼ ✳ ✥

Is it ____ ____ ____ ____ ____ ?
✼ ☆ ✧ ★ ✶

Is it ____ ____ ____ ____ ____ ?
✯ ✭ ✛ ✪ ✥

Is it ____ ____ ____ ____ ____ ____ ?
✪ ✭ ✷ ✥ ✪ ✹

"ADMIRABLE" IS VERY GOOD, TO BE ADMIRED.

Is it ____ ____ ____ ____ ____ ____ ____ ____ ____ ?
✡ ♣ ✬ ☆ ✼ ✡ ✛ ✪ ✥

CODE: A ✡ D ♣ G ✧ I ☆ M ✬ O ✭ R ✼ T ✶ V ✷ B ✛ E ✥ H ★ L ✪ N ✯ P ✰ S ✳ U ✳ Y ✹

SINCERE WORDS AND AN HONEST HEART

VALUE BUILDERS
CONVICTION & SINCERITY

✎ **The words to the Bible verse, Job 33:3, make a path through this word search. Draw a line to follow the words and then write them in the spaces below.**

START

M Y W O R D S C B B B L I P S S B B B B B B B B B

B B B B B B B O B B B Y B B B I B B B B B B B B B

B B B B B B B M B B T M B B B N B B B B B B B B B

B B B M O R F E B B R B B B B C B B B B I K N O W

B B B A B B B B B B A B B B B E B B B B T B B B B

B B B N B B B B B B E B B B B R B B B B A B B B B

B B B U P R I G H T H B B B B E B B B B H B B B B

B B B B B B B B B B B B B B B L B B B B W B B B B

B B B B B B B B B B B B B B B Y S P E A K B B B B

B B B B B B B B B B B B B B B B B B B B B B B B B

M Y   _ _ _ _ _   _ _ _ _ _

_ _ _ _   _ _   _ _ _ _ _ _ _

_ _ _ _ _ ;   M Y   _ _ _ _ _

S I N C E R E L Y   _ _ _ _ _

_ _ _ _   I   _ _ _ _ _ . Job 33:3

"UPRIGHT" MEANS HONEST.

What does it mean to have an honest heart? ______________________________

____

MAKE A STORY TUBE ABOUT SINCERITY

Can you use pictures to tell a story about your most sincere friend?

You need:

- ☐ Empty paper towel roll
- ☐ Scissors
- ☐ 2 craft sticks
- ☐ White paper
- ☐ Pencil and markers
- ☐ Ruler
- ☐ Glue or tape

To make a Story Tube:

1. Cut a 2" piece of the tube off of one end.
2. Glue or tape 1 craft stick to the 2 pieces of tube so the cut off piece is reattached, but now about 1/4" away from the longer end of the tube. Glue the second craft stick beside the first one.
3. Cut a strip of paper 1-1/2" x 10". Draw a line every 2" to make 5 boxes on the paper.
4. Draw pictures to tell a story about your most sincere friend. Be sure to include ways your friend shows his or her sincerity.

To use your Story Tube:

1. Put the strip of paper into the slot with the first picture framed in the tube.
2. Point the tube toward a light or window.
3. Slide the pictures along in the slot to show your story.
4. Make other stories using longer or shorter pieces of paper as needed.

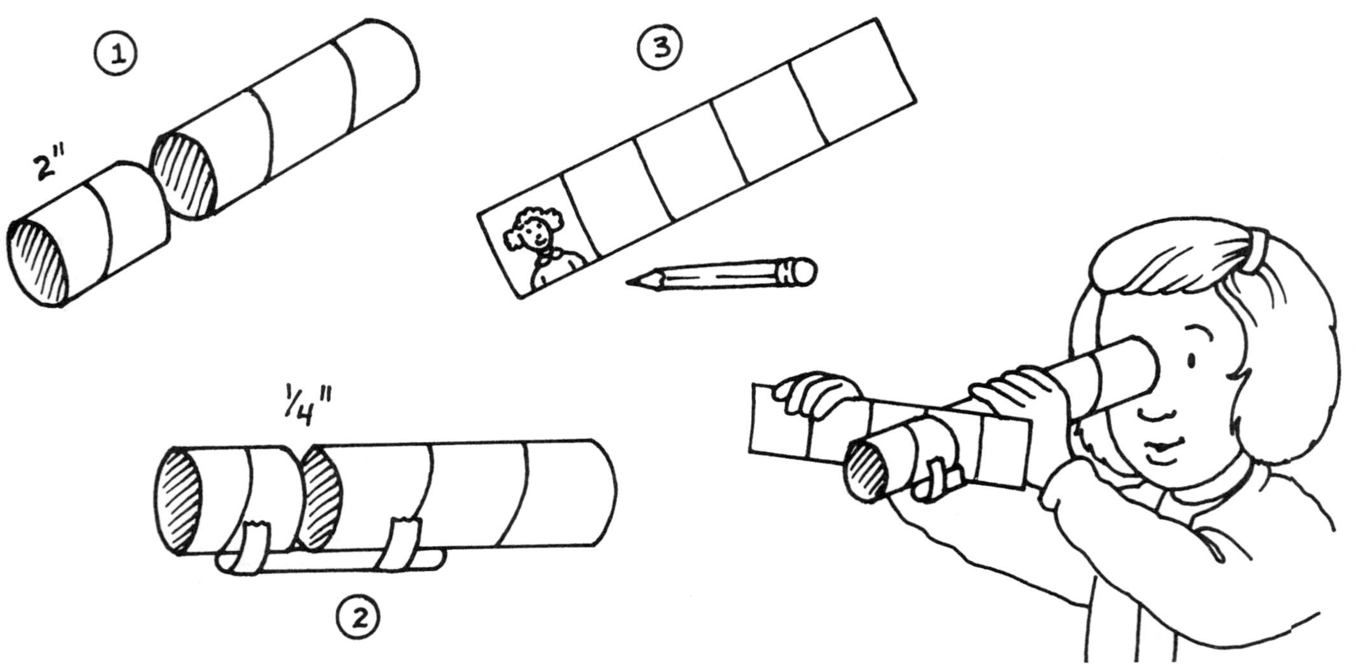

COMPLIMENTS

VALUE BUILDERS
CONVICTION & SINCERITY

A compliment is saying something good or nice about someone. Everyone likes a compliment—if it is sincere. But sometimes people may give a compliment to get something in return. This is the opposite of being sincere. ✎ **Look at what's happening in each cartoon strip, then write your answers to the questions that follow each.**

Was Tammy's compliment sincere or not? ________________

How do you think Brad felt when Tammy asked to copy his homework?

____

Was Cameron being sincere?__________________

How do you think Cameron's words made his grandma feel?

____

How can you tell when a compliment is not sincere?

____

IS THIS SINCERITY OR NOT?

Do you say, "I'll help do the dishes!" when you are thinking, "If I help with the dishes, no one will make me do my spelling for school"? Is this being sincere?

✎ **See the letter at the top of each line? Follow the line and write that letter in the box at the end to find out more about sincerity.**

SINCERITY
IS NOT

SINCERITY
IS

T E D I E G N P R N Y I N A S G T E U R

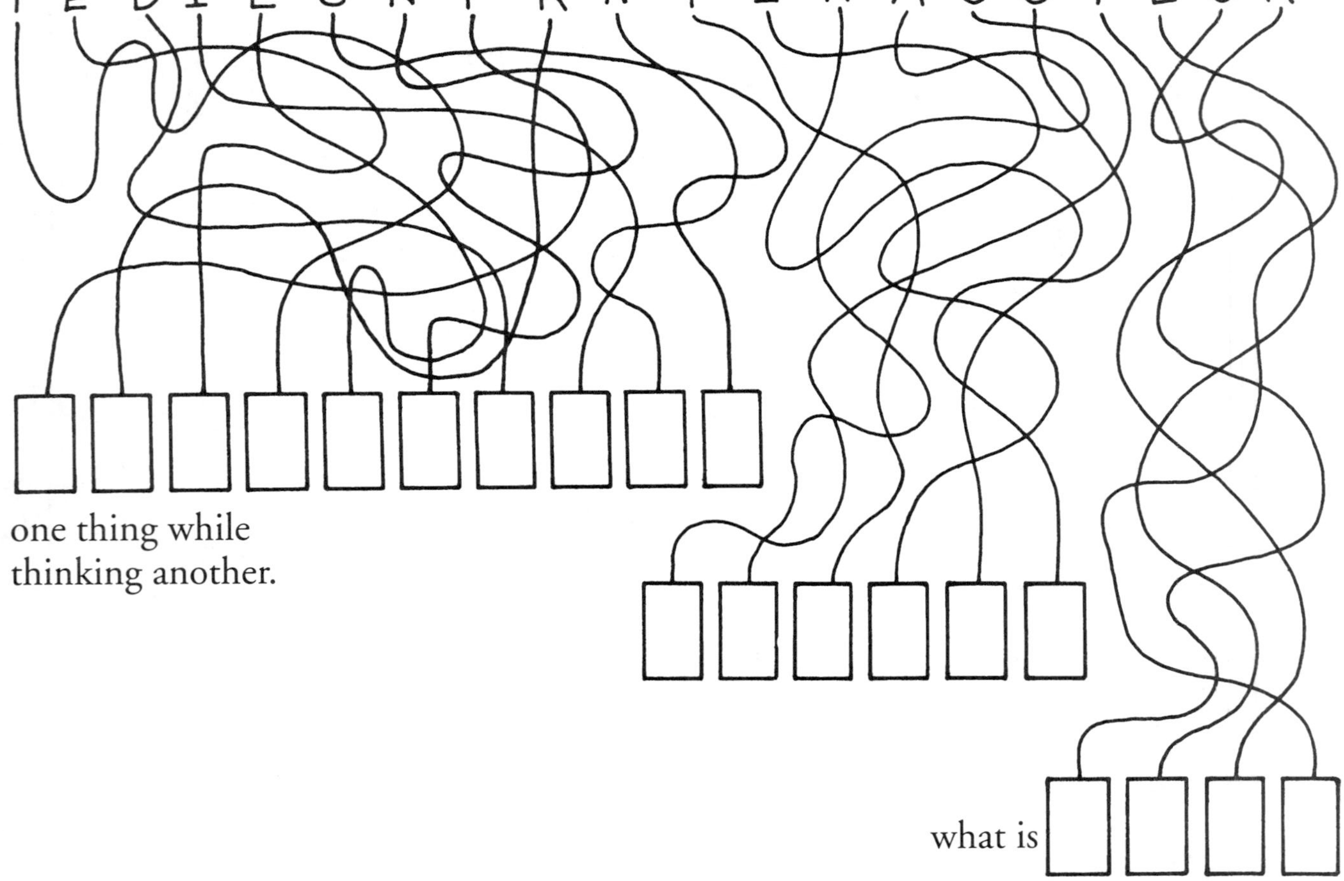

one thing while
thinking another.

what is

BEING SINCERE WITH NOTHING TO HIDE

VALUE BUILDERS
CONVICTION & SINCERITY

✎ **Can you find the sincere faces? There are thirteen of them hidden in the picture below. Circle each one, then color the picture.**

Remember: Sincerity is saying and doing what is true without pretending or hiding anything.

VALUE BUILDERS
CONVICTION & SINCERITY

THE BIBLE TELLS ABOUT SINCERITY

Timothy Is Sincere about Believing in Jesus

The Apostle Paul wrote letters to Timothy. Paul loved Timothy as if he were his son and wanted to be with Timothy when it was possible.

2 Timothy 1:1-7; 3:14, 15; 1 Timothy 1:1, 2; 4:10-16

"INFANCY" MEANS WHEN SOMEONE IS A BABY.

[From] Paul . . .
To Timothy . . .
I thank God . . . as night and day I constantly remember you in my prayers. Recalling your tears, I long to see you, so that I may be filled with joy. I have been reminded of your sincere faith, which first lived in your grandmother Lois and in your mother Eunice and, I am persuaded, now lives in you also. For this reason I remind you to fan into flame the gift of God, which is in you through the laying on of my hands. For God did not give us a spirit of timidity, but a spirit of power, of love and of self-discipline. . . .

"RECALLING" IS REMEMBERING.

But as for you, continue in what you have learned and have become convinced of, because you know those from whom you learned it, and how from infancy you have known the holy Scriptures, which are able to make you wise for salvation through faith in Christ Jesus.

(Read the rest of this story on page 39)

✎ **Draw a picture of the people in this story. Then draw a line from the picture to the sentences that tell about that person.**

Eunice	Timothy	Paul	Lois

I am a grandmother.
I was pleased to share my faith in Jesus with my family.

My family taught me about the Bible when I was very young.
I keep serving Jesus with an honest and sincere faith.

I am very glad to be the mother of a young man who knows Jesus.
We read the Bible to our children starting when they were babies.

I write lots of letters to help my friends know more about Jesus.

THE BIBLE TELLS ABOUT BEING SINCERE

Timothy Is Sincere about Believing in Jesus

(2 Timothy 1:1-7; 3:14, 15; 1 Timothy 1:1, 2; 4:10-16 continued from page 38)

[From] Paul, an apostle of Christ Jesus . . .

To Timothy my true son in the faith . . .

We have put our hope in the living God, who is the Savior of all men, and especially of those who believe.

Command and teach these things. Don't let anyone look down on you because you are young, but set an example for the believers in speech, in life, in love, in faith and in purity. Until I come, devote yourself to the public reading of Scripture, to preaching and to teaching. . . .

Be diligent in these matters; give yourself wholly to them, so that everyone may see your progress. Watch your life and doctrine closely. Persevere in them, because if you do, you will save both yourself and your hearers.

✎ **Use the code to fill in the blanks.**

In his letters, Paul asked Timothy to . . .

1. Keep ________ (☐) the things ________ (○) had given him the ________ (☆) to do.

2. Remember what he ________ (⬭) about the ________ (▭) when he was a ________ (△) ________ (◇).

3. Do ________ (✕) that show other ________ (⬡) what being a ________ (⌂) is like.

☆ = *ability* ▭ = *Bible* ◇ = *boy* ⌂ = *Christian* ☐ = *doing* ○ = *God*
⬭ = *learned* △ = *little* ⬡ = *people* ✕ = *things*

LETTERS TO TIMOTHY

✎ **Timothy has been getting lots of mail and needs your help. Read each letter and answer as you think Timothy may have.**

Dear Timothy,
I like learning about you because I have also lived in a Christian family my whole life. I started hearing about God before I could even talk. (That's what my Dad says. Sometimes my Mom says she wishes I hadn't learned to talk quite so well—or at least so loud.)
My question to you is this: Is it really important to act like a Christian even when you're with lots of kids that don't know Jesus?
Thanks,
Jerome

Dear Jerome,
I'm glad you have a Christian family. My answer to your question is YES and NO.
YES, because you ARE a Christian. If you don't live your life in a way that you know is right, then you are not being true to yourself. In other words, you are not being SINCERELY you! But, NO, if you are only acting like a Christian to show off or make the other kids feel bad. That would be pretending. I hope this helps.
Write again,
Timothy

DEAR TIMMY,
DO YOU HAVE A PET FROG? I'D SEND YOU MY BROTHER BUT I NEED HIM. I'M SINCERE ABOUT THIS.

Dear Timothy,
Paul said you had "sincere" faith. What did he mean? I want to be like you, since I am young like you were.
Love,
Duke

Dear Duke,
____
____
____
____
____

MAKE A BIBLE VERSE GAME

VALUE BUILDERS
CONVICTION & SINCERITY

Make a magnet game and learn the words of this Bible verse in Hebrews 10:22. "Let us draw near to God with a sincere heart."

You need:

- ☐ (6) colored 3" x 5" cards cut into 3" x 2-1/2" cards
- ☐ 11 chenille wires
- ☐ Pencil
- ☐ Markers
- ☐ Gift box lid, about 9" x 15"
- ☐ Magnet
- ☐ OPTIONAL: 11 paper clips, tape or glue

✂ **To make a Bible Verse Game:**

1. Fold each 3" x 2-1/2" card in half.
2. Use the marker to write each word of the Bible verse on a separate card. Write the same word on each side of the card.
3. Cut each chenille wire in half, then curl each half around the pencil to make two coils.
4. Insert a folded word card into each pair of coiled wires to make a game piece.
5. Put all the game pieces into the box lid.

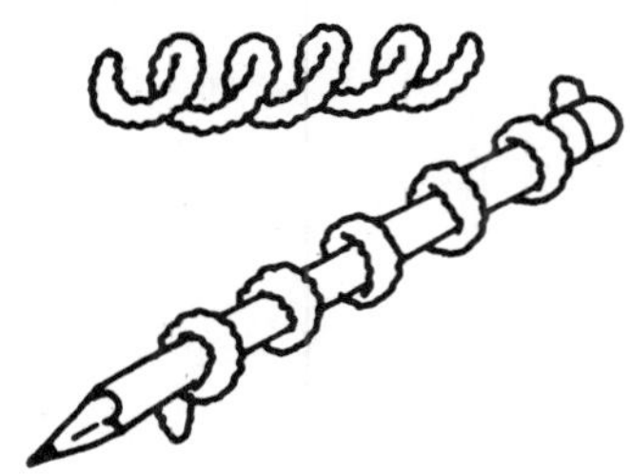

✂ **To play your Bible Verse Game:**

1. Move the magnet around UNDER the lid to move each game piece.
2. Move the game pieces on the box lid so the Bible verse can be read with the words in order.
3. Use a kitchen timer to see how long it takes to put the game pieces in order.
4. Scramble the pieces and then see if you can beat your best time.
5. OPTIONAL: If the magnet does not easily move the game pieces, glue or tape a paper clip to the bottom of each coiled wire.

THE VALUE OF SINCERITY

God's values are the STANDARD to help me to know how to live my life and treat other people

HOW CAN YOU KNOW WHAT YOUR VALUES ARE?

Look at the things you DO, SAY, and THINK. If you spend time doing something, then you know it is one of your values.

Are you thinking what is in the thought balloon?

My name is ______________________________

Being sincere ______________ important to me.
is   is not

I ______________ spend time saying and doing what is true, without
do   do not
pretending or hiding anything.

Doing and saying what is true, without hiding anything, is sincerity.

I can show that sincerity is becoming my value when I ____________________

____________________________ and ______________________________

✎ **Write and/or draw a TV commercial about a TV show in which the characters are sincere to one another.**

VALUE BUILDERS SERIES INDEX
BY VALUE

VALUE BUILDERS
CONVICTION & SINCERITY

Accepting
Romans 15:7
Galatians 3:28
Luke 7 Jesus and the woman with no name
Acts 10 Peter's vision and visit

Appreciative
See thankful

Attentive
Psalm 34:15
James 1:19
Nehemiah 8 Ezra reads the law
Luke 10 Mary listens to Jesus

Caring
See concerned

Choices
See wise

Committed
1 Kings 8:61
Proverbs 16:3
Esther 4 Esther
John 1 Andrew follows Jesus

Compassionate
2 Corinthians 1:3-4
1 Peter 3:8
Luke 10 Good Samaritan
Luke 23 Jesus on the cross

Concerned
1 Corinthians 12:25
1 John 3:17
Matthew 25 Jesus teaches to meet needs
Acts 2 Church provides for each other

Confident
Philippians 4:13
Psalm 139:14
1 Samuel 17 David and Goliath
Nehemiah 6 Nehemiah isn't intimidated

Considerate
See respectful, kind

Consistent
1 John 3:18
Psalm 33:4
Matthew 26 Jesus in the garden
Daniel 6 Daniel as administrator

Contented
See peaceful

Conviction
Deuteronomy 13:6-8
Acts 4:19-20
Daniel 3 Blazing furnace and three Hebrews
John 2 Jesus clears the temple courts

Cooperative
Colossians 3:23-24
Ephesians 4:16
Acts 6 Disciples share responsibilities
Exodus 18 Jethro gives Moses a plan

Courageous
Joshua 1:9
Isaiah 41:10
Acts 23 Paul's nephew
Esther 4 Esther

Creative
See resourceful

Decision Making
See purposeful

Dedicated
See committed

Dependable
See responsible

Diligent
See persevering, purposeful, responsible

Discerning
See wise

Discipleship
See teachable, prayerful, worshipful, faith, holy

Discipline
See self-disciplined

Empathy
Galatians 6:2
Hebrews 13:3
John 11 Jesus at Lazarus's death
1 Samuel 19 Jonathan speaks up for David

Endurance
See persevering, self-disciplined, purposeful

Enthusiasm
See joyful

Fairness
Leviticus 19:15
Romans 12:17
James 2 Favoritism at a meeting
Matthew 20 Parable of workers

Faith
John 3:16
Hebrews 11:6
Acts 16 Philippian jailer
Matthew 8 Centurion sends servant to Jesus

Faithful
See loyal

VALUE BUILDERS SERIES INDEX

BY VALUE

VALUE BUILDERS SERIES INDEX
BY VALUE

Merciful
Psalm 103:10
Micah 6:8
1 Samuel 25 — Abigail helps David show mercy
Matthew 18 — Unmerciful servant

Obedient
See also respectful
1 Samuel 15:22
Ephesians 6:1
1 Samuel 17 — David takes lunch
Acts 9 — Ananias at Saul's conversion

Patience
Psalm 37: 7
Ephesians 4:2
Genesis 26 — Isaac opens new wells
Nehemiah 6 — Nehemiah stands firm

Peaceful
John 14:27
Hebrews 13:5-6
Acts 12 — Peter sleeping in prison
Matthew 6 — Jesus teaches contentment

Peer pressure, response to
See confident, conviction, wise

Persevering
Galatians 6:9
James 1:2-3
Acts 27 — Paul in shipwreck
Exodus 5 — Moses doesn't give up

Praise
See prayerful, thankful, worshipful

Prayerful
Philippians 4:6
James 5:16
Luke 11 — Jesus teaches disciples
Daniel 6 — Daniel prays daily

Pure
See holy

Purposeful
James 1:22
1 Corinthians 15:58
Matthew 26 — Jesus in Gethsemane
Joshua 24 — Joshua serves God

Reliable
See responsible

Repentant
Acts 26:20
1 John 1:9
Luke 15 — Prodigal son
Luke 22 — Peter's denial

Resourceful
Philippians 4:9
1 Peter 4:10
Luke 5 — Man lowered through roof
Luke 19 — Zacchaeus

Respectful
Deuteronomy 5:16
1 Peter 2:17
1 Samuel 26 — David doesn't kill Saul
Acts 16 — Lydia and other believers

Responsible
Galatians 6:4-5
Proverbs 20:11
Acts 20 — Paul continues his work
Numbers 13 — Caleb follows instructions

Reverence
Daniel 6:26-27
Psalm 78:4, 7
Daniel 3 — Blazing furnace and three Hebrews
Matthew 21 — Triumphal entry

Self-controlled
See self-disciplined

Self-disciplined
1 Timothy 4:7-8
2 Timothy 1:7
Daniel 1 — Daniel and king's meat
John 19 — Jesus was mocked

Self-esteem
See confident

Sensitivity
See empathy, compassionate, concerned, kind

Service (servanthood)
See cooperative, generosity, helpful, stewardship

Sharing
See generosity, stewardship

Sincerity
Romans 12:9
Job 33:3
Mark 5 — Jairus and his daughter
2 Timothy 1 — Timothy

Stewardship
Luke 3:11
Ephesians 5:15-16
2 Chronicles 31 — Temple contributions
Acts 4 — Believers share

Submission
See humble, respectful, self-disciplined

Supportive
See friendly, loving

VALUE BUILDERS SERIES INDEX

BY VALUE

VALUE BUILDERS SERIES INDEX
BY SCRIPTURE

VALUE BUILDERS SERIES INDEX

BY SCRIPTURE